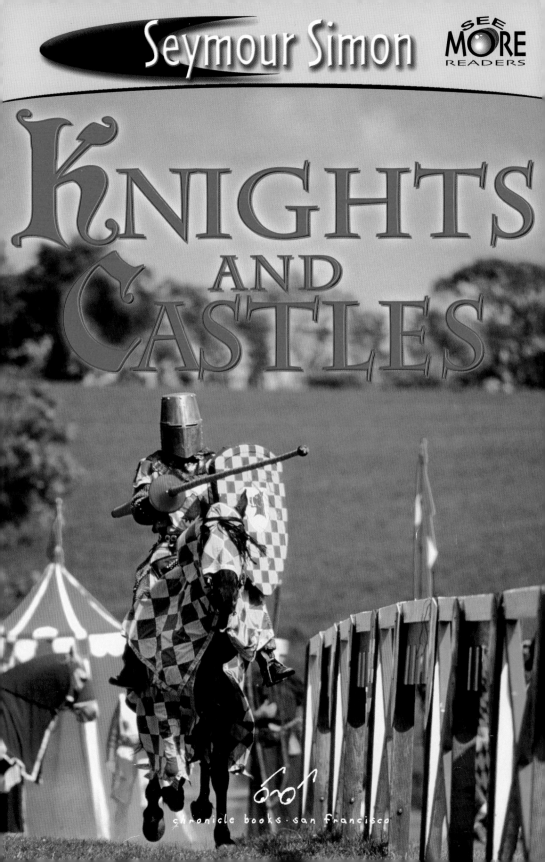

Seymour Simon

SEE MORE READERS

Knights and Castles

chronicle books · san francisco

To my son Rob, who had his own toy castle when he was young.

The author especially thanks David Reuther and Ellen Friedman for their thoughtful editorial and design suggestions as well as their enthusiasm for the SeeMore Readers. Also, many thanks to Victoria Rock, Beth Weber, Molly Glover, Tracy Johnson, and Nancy Tran at Chronicle Books for their generous assistance and support of these books.

Permission to use the following photographs is gratefully acknowledged:
Front cover: © J. M. Mata/iStockphoto; page 1: © Pete Dancs/Getty Images; page 3 © Stan Levy/Photo Researchers, Inc.; pages 4–5: © Michael Krasowitz/Getty Images; page 6–7 and 34–35: © Charles & Josette Lenars/CORBIS; pages 9, 15, 20–21, and back cover: © England's Medieval Festival at Herstmonceux Castle, East Sussex, England http://www.medievalimagebank.com/; pages 10–11: © Erik Von Weber/Getty Images; pages 12–13: © Richard T. Nowitz/CORBIS; page 16: © Kenneth C. Zirkel/iStockphoto, pages 18–19: © Ira Block/Getty Images; pages 22–23: © Franz-Marc Frei/COR-BIS; pages 24–25: © Patrick Ward/CORBIS; pages 26–27: © Georg Gerster/Photo Researchers, Inc.; page 29: © Debi Gardiner/iStockphoto; pages 30–31:© Peter Adams/Getty Images; pages 32–33: © Robert Holmes/CORBIS; page 37: © Richard Price/Getty Images ; pages 38–39: © Gavin Hellier/Getty Images; page 40: © Rafael Macia/Photo Researchers, Inc.

Book design by Ellen Friedman.
Typeset in 16-point ITC Century Book.
Manufactured in China.

Library of Congress Cataloging-in-Publication Data
Simon, Seymour.
Knights and castles / Seymour Simon.
p. cm. — (SeeMore readers)
ISBN-13: 978-0-8118-5408-5 (library edition)
ISBN-10: 0-8118-5408-6 (library edition)
ISBN-13: 978-0-8118-5409-2 (pbk.)
ISBN-10: 0-8118-5409-4 (pbk.)
1. Castles. 2. Knights and knighthood. I. Title.
GT3520.S56 2006
940—dc22
2005027568

Distributed in Canada by Raincoast Books
9050 Shaughnessy Street, Vancouver, British Columbia V6P 6E5

10 9 8 7 6 5 4 3 2 1

Chronicle Books LLC
85 Second Street, San Francisco, California 94105

www.chroniclekids.com

A thousand years ago in Europe, kings and their wealthy landowners, called lords, lived in large, stone houses called castles. The lords and their best soldiers lived in these castles, which were built to keep out enemies.

The soldiers were called knights. They wore armor and rode horses into battle. Knights lived during a time called the Middle Ages, a period of about 500 years between the ancient and modern times in Europe.

When a knight fought, he wore a heavy suit of metal armor. The armor protected the knight from swords, arrows, spears, and other weapons.

A group of knights attacking on horseback was a scary sight. They were like the armored tanks used in modern warfare. The knights could easily defeat enemy foot soldiers who wore no armor.

But if a knight fell or was knocked from his horse, he was in trouble. The armor was so heavy that he could not rise from the ground without help.

In the early part of the Middle Ages, knights wore long shirts made of leather or heavy cloth. Over that, they wore suits of chain mail, made from small metal rings linked together.

Each piece of armor was specially made to fit the knight's body. The knight wore a simple metal helmet. He wore a collar made of chain mail to protect his neck. And he wore metal shoes, and gloves called gauntlets.

These early knights rode on horses, but the horses usually had no armor. On horseback, a knight carried a long spear called a lance and a large shield that protected most of his body.

In later times, helmets covered the knight's entire head. Most helmets had pointed fronts to turn aside a blow from a lance or a sword. They had small openings for the knight to see and breathe through. And the fronts of the helmets had visors that could be lifted up and down.

Pieces of metal plate covered the knight's arms and legs. By the 1400s, knights were wearing whole suits of armor. A knight had to be strong to wear armor that weighed about 50 pounds or more.

A boy chosen to become a knight left home when he was only 7 years old and went to live as a page in the house of a knight or the castle of a lord. There he learned to ride horses and use weapons. He also learned a knight's code of behavior. A knight was expected to protect women and the weak, to serve his lord and the king, and to defend the church, even with his life.

At the age of about 14, a page became a squire. As a squire, he continued training with weapons, learned to hunt with falcons, cared for the knight's horse, cleaned the stables, polished the armor, and rode with the knight into battle. At the age of 21, a squire would go through a religious ceremony to become a knight, and receive his own sword and armor.

When they wore armor during a battle, knights looked very much alike. So each knight had his own coat of arms, an emblem made of colors, symbols, and drawings of real or mythological [MYTH-o-lodge-ical] animals. A coat of arms was worn on the knight's shield and helmet and often on a standard or banner. Only knights had coats of arms, and they were passed down to the sons of the knight.

The people who knew one coat of arms from another were called heralds. Heralds were used to carry messages between lords and their knights, and they had to know a friend from a foe. Heraldry is the study of coats of arms and the history of the families that used them.

Lances and swords were not the only kinds of weapons used during the Middle Ages. To battle knights in armor, foot soldiers used spears with long handles called pikes, as well as crossbows and longbows.

A crossbow is a small bow fixed to a stock of wood like a rifle. The bowstring is released by a trigger.

Longbows were first used in battle in the 1300s. A trained archer could fire 12 arrows a minute. He could wound an enemy at 250 yards, kill at 100 yards, and pierce a knight's armor at 60 yards. The longbow became the most important weapon of the Middle Ages.

Sometimes a lord would arrange a tournament where knights fought against each other in jousts [JOW-sts]. In early jousts, two groups of knights chased each other over a large open field and tried to knock opponents off their horses with lances or swords. Injuries and even deaths were common.

Later in the Middle Ages, knights fought each other one on one. Separated by over 100 yards, knights would charge each other until one of them was unhorsed.

Crowds of people gathered to watch knights jousting and archery contests at these tournaments. Today, "medieval" fairs often feature jousts as a main attraction.

The word *castle* comes from a Latin word for an ancient Roman fort. People have been building castles and forts for more than 5,000 years.

Early forts had walls made of earth and later of wood that were circled by ditches. The fort's defenders stood on the top of the walls, hurling stones and spears at the enemy.

Many stone castles were built in Europe during the Middle Ages. Most of the castles had walls built with 3 thick layers: an outer layer of stone, a filling of earth and stones, and a stone inner shell. Some castles have walls 10 or more feet thick.

Towers were built along the wall, and a large, strong tower known as a keep was often built inside the wall. Paths along the tops of the walls connected the towers. Openings in the walls alongside the paths allowed defenders to shoot arrows or throw boiling water at the enemy below.

The castle was not only a fortress but a prison as well. Dark, damp underground dungeons held prisoners who were often kept in chains.

Moats were added around castles for extra protection. Many castles were built on the banks of rivers or lakes, and water was channeled into the moats. Other moats were filled with rainfall.

A drawbridge lay across a moat and could be raised or lowered as needed. If an enemy made it across the moat, there were still several sets of heavy metal gates to block the entrance to the castle.

Every castle had a great hall where the lord and his family dined. They also held large banquets [BANK-wets] for many guests, where they were entertained by singers and musicians.

The great hall was lit with torches and heated by large fireplaces built into the walls. Large pieces of fabric called tapestries [TAP-ess-trees] were hung over the walls, but the floor was usually bare and covered with straw.

It was difficult to capture a castle.
The enemy would try to make holes in
the castle walls using catapults. A catapult
was like a huge slingshot that flings heavy
rocks against the walls. Attackers also used
battering rams, wooden towers on wheels,
and ladders to climb over the walls.

If all else failed, the enemy might surround the castle and try to starve out the people inside. If the siege lasted for only a few weeks, the defenders had a good chance of surviving. But if the siege went on for many months, the defenders might run out of food and have to surrender.

Castles were built to defend against sieges from enemy knights. But with the invention of gunpowder and cannons, castle building began to change. Gunpowder exploded with enough power to knock down even the strongest walls.

By the 1400s some castles were built of brick rather than stone. These were used as houses rather than forts. The lords of these castles did not expect a siege nor did they keep armies of knights. The Middle Ages were drawing to a close and the period known as the Renaissance [REN-uh-sonce] was beginning, bringing new ideas in science and art.

Castles and huge stone fortresses were built in many other parts of the world besides Europe. There are castles and forts along the African coast, in the Middle East, in South and Central America, in India, in Korea, and in Japan.

Indian castles and forts were built in the last few hundred years. In India, elephants rather than horses were used to fight in battles, so the gates to an Indian castle were high enough for an elephant to pass through.

In Japan, castles date back to the late 1500s. Japanese castles, like the one on the left, were built on stone bases, but the upper floors were usually made of wood and plaster. Japanese warriors, called samurai [SAM-ur-I], wore armor and used swords, bows, and arrows.

Today, people enjoy visiting castles to see how life was in the Middle Ages. Many castles have old weapons and suits of armor on display. Visitors are sometimes able to attend a banquet in the great hall and walk into the dungeons. Old castles are still a source of wonder around the world.